LAZARUS AT HIS DESK

HARRY EDGAR PALACIO

LAZARUS AT HIS DESK

VERTIGO-TALK

CYCLE I

atmosphere press

© 2025 Harry Edgar Palacio

Published by Atmosphere Press

Cover design by Ronaldo Alves

No part of this book may be reproduced without permission from the author except in brief quotations and in reviews.

Atmospherepress.com

For kalki, dad and mom

One day, I decided to steal some.
I pocketed one grain.
The snow glowed bluely in my hovel.
My little lamp.
Then one night I don't know why I swallowed it.
And this is what I saw."
   -Cathy Park Hong

"Now what seas, what meanings
can I place in you?"
   -Mary Szybist

CONTENTS

Waking Life	1
Awake	3
Carro Publico	4
Airport/ In Transit	5
Terminals	6
Passengers	7
Sleepless Travel	8
O' Progeny	9
Ancestral Dysmorphia	11
Oracle-bloodline	12
Brevity	14
Ayer	15
Intimations	16
Plainsong	17
Pause	18
Eurydice	19
Pyres	20
Invisible Creatures	21
Abbreviated Space	23
Jazz Scriptures	24
Puja of Bodywork	25
Fine Lines	26
Inertia	27
New Mythology	29
Amnesiacs on a Schedule	30
Hard Candy	31
Juggling	33
Earworm	34
Childlike	35
Code-Switch	36
Tiny Parakeet	37
Lifecycle of Stars	38

Light Work	39
Stars and/or Gods	40
Driving Blind	41
Saffron-touch	42
Sapphire Clouds	43
Sepia Light	44
Feral Headlights	45
Nude Gem	46
Glow	47
Hopscotch	48
Cinema	49
PDA like the Half-life of a Plum	51
Night Vision	52
Anthology of Ancient Anxieties	54
Rivers of Elysium	55
Catacombs	57
Island of Tangents	58
Pedro Páramo's Phantoms	59
Strange Bats	60
Catalog	61
Mecca	62
Indigo Village	63
Phylum of Jazz	64
Mulatto Colony	65
Isolation	66
Escaping	67
Scriptwriter	68
Hazel Heat	69
Hiss of Paranoia	70
Green Wanderings	71
Arrowhead Thoughts	72
Strange Eternities	73
Afterthought	74
Afterthought Cycle	75

Waking Life

In the slow cascade where neon becomes a part of our bodies; people lingering. A familiar song follows you home again. Circling us, our bodies are empires of ephemera. A labyrinth of amber flows from pores. Silent breath squeezed shut compressed by fallow lips. A year of isolation turns into two and a half. Measured by the weight of books stacked against a wall. As gestation weighs heavier or becomes lightness and gravity in nightfall clasping tiny hands across enumerable invisible cities. Slow immaculate Jazz pries rain from clouds. A snake-rattle crackling dark-skinned, omen-eyed shaman to sleep in a laundry room somewhere out west. Sleepwalking through the ebb and flow, thought like a talisman: we exist through a retelling, our mutual history, we are shared skin. This is what becomes of us when our hands remove cerulean smoke from a ghost-memory. Talking to yourself so you can hear people-breath, a psalm that sometimes becomes stranger's words following you throughout history.

"The path to paradise begins in hell"
 - *Dante Aligheiri*

Awake

Lazarus longingly cares for his own foreign forget; his past life
The afterthought of death looming like weaving loops of cursive.
Dilating bulbs climbing the perspiring catacombs.
A sleep that was handed down by a pandemic and Masons, a
sallow fever-like complexion. A half-gold helix of natural order
moving through the finite nature of a terrestrial body.

Lazarus rising, his hand still clasping the carpenter's calloused but
perfect fingers as though sent down from a celestial place.
Breath enters and finds him, fills his lungs with damp air.
Dusk meets those searching for *what else but* god, cerulean sleep
without face or memory of being.
Its cool reminder of earth and dust lingering like heady saplings
wavering in the wind drunk on mirth.

Carro Publico (Public Car)

There are so many half-open books of human lives, those pear-shaped bodies with dangling trinkets, kumkum and dogeared memory flickering from one life to the next, passing ostensibly by as though bodies were a fortress nestled with spirit, fragrant as jasmine. With the strange fright of fire, blooming by the parapet of the city's rooftops, the past a mirage of sitar plucked as though we were speaking in swift abrasive sign language. Time rolled down the chin of our longing, not recognizing lost syrupy dollops being turned into photographs on refrigerator doors telling aging myths where god stood invisible to one side refracting light in just the right way. An omen of wisdoms where the brute, protruding wrinkles were a cross you bore reminding others you've lived long enough to forget a few things. Stony in the night temple. The words repeated themselves like ribbons of skein and a thimble working an eyelet of a needle. I took a *carro publico* jammed with people, the raw smell of sweat lacquered with the sound of bachata- we were threaded through the city of Santo Domingo like cats gnawing at cryptic blankets. Dazedly picking up the receiver: she heard the storytelling like strange bats hurling themselves blindly at birds. We parted like a lamp bulb finally burnt out to think you can be like a dethroned prince who never forgets he was royalty. Lingering in night insomnia is a reminder that you've had a good life, days are at your beck- This may be a cyclical existence in the violet storm of night, we can weigh the ebb and flow as though a cistern were slowly filling with explanations.

Airport/ In Transit

"Be not forgetful to entertain strangers: for there by some have entertained angels unawares."   *-Hebrews 13:2*

As in the descent to the Turkish airport/ a diorama of cigarette butts in a ventilated room/ moon music/ real isolation with friends, coffee, and dark-chocolate/ Turkish currency to bring home/ no re-enter clause: I just want to see the moon buildings, the craters of edifices perched like protracted wombs/ the Phoenician sunset/ the dialogue of women and men, the strange custodians of culture and dialects as I ask the unfathomable questions of time: who are we?/ Tourists walking frenetically through airports/ a loading shipyard to Tibet or Beijing?/ maybe the sky falls a bit/ dregs of light like new skin/ slightly overhangs beige silhouettes/ 6-7 arms 8-9 legs formless head(s) like the lord Vishnu himself here in Istanbul/ surreal like the nude traces of travel: a bedroom with a dutiful clock, sienna hands touching and/or not touching yours/ off white pigment ergo skin/ comes like vertigo a tempest leaving the white, fuchsia glow of stars like pulpy sky fire/ something about this nonplussed conversation feels like there is only a tiny exit area left and an amniotic fluid-sac-to feed and breathe into until we make peace with eternity.

Terminals

A snake-like row of lines snapping their corpulent fingers onto a snare-drum of anima/ fumbling purposeful, popping in and out of traffic, tenuous reminders of sleep being overridden. Live bats peeking their fingers into the bathhouses of a snow country. Face up at a desk wrestling with argonauts, white noise inflames a palm of amorphous terminals, travelers plugging away at stasis as though being conscious reminds us repeatedly of being in a singular place. Working at the bruise with a phantom maw until its indigo hue opens pomegranate skin cupping arils, we have plucked the weight of isolation, every diode and consumed its incarnadine kernels. Falling in ether is like floating in amniotic fluid. I have thought of being consumed by flames, lapsing breath as age unspools, an unclasping of skin, body, and night-time considerations.

Passengers

Red lights puff, a preening glow
Let hands cool in a well, mystery tucked in our smile
Collecting heartache by the mounds then forgetting
What stripes red or blue would best run down
Eager backs of nautical bodies?
Naked passing time forgetting youth runs from us.
Side glances to capture its escaping light
Wading ankle deep in froths of time, a bent posture
Where we dive headfirst into a dying rivulet
We are glass animals pieced together by omniscient hands
Bird-like wings jutting out from our torso we return to a lake of splendor
Weighing winter on skin slivers of work baring itself
And we undress, ask gods for privacy, become awkward-lovers
We are new strangers facing a mirror daily; old children
We had closed our eyes, there was a dint in the window
Pecking noises had begun to die down,
A mind tending to an astronomical task,
We cast off paper boats out to sail and just this once we were passengers.

Sleepless Travel

A room of pale fire, its silences a soft, olive-skin light. An island of fecund highways, dilating fingers traveling over invisible cities. We come to seek your hybrid movements. A river caught in sallow hands its rumination slipping through you slowly capsizing and emptying itself, a simulation of passing on from this life. A wan sleepless timbre of fluid limbs trying to hold onto a past life. We go back and forth with ghosts giving them spaces in unimaginable longing, they send us to the outer reaches of the Himalayas. Its windfall that of finding nude places along our amber skin which brings consciousness back to our breath. We often do not see fruits of what we sow until we taste it in our mouths salivating; bee combs perspiring honey. I am wondering what is arising in this long remainder of days ahead, a waiting room where a stranger sits beside you. An afternoon of howls, awareness glowing like golden teeth working marrow. Wondering who this person is, telling you everything about your life lived; remembering a long time into the future you had sent us here to gaze as though a reflection. A stranger thing to be conscious of death. Time passes unlike here on earth. Sometimes life changes us as though we were meant to be changed. We live and die as though maps of secret cities, beyond comprehension.

O' Progeny

"And Enoch walked with God: and he was not; for God took him."
-Genesis 5:24

She clipped it from the branch its incarnadine hue like the sunsetting on those auspicious days we seldom see, the phone rang then silence then rang again waiting to hear a voice from afar. Strung together like pearls sent adrift by girls newly ending adolescence the euphony of angel song latched from hip to hip to unnamed peopling, the soft speaker gathering distance a space between an impenetrable fortress of earth like the national debt rising to unreachable precipices, a dial winding down counterclockwise where we read history like birds migrating to their summer homes. I have thought of loss as a way to gain access to a society; a race: those forlorn hands, their canine teeth facing the sun, aquatic movements in the bath of wolf-dreams, their sanguine touch in perilous questioning, ramparts tressed in Sanskrit glyphs, oblations to nomadic gods, there is a foyer where a mirror hangs like a reminder that we are who we say we are as we enter the white building composing ourselves before the stairs, the question remains am I the body that keeps changing year after year like the continual pruning of leaves falling from a Red Maple, we are the earth as volcanic women teach their alphabet tongues, a language of kiss and sometimes tell to the lucky ones. A quotidian task of gratitude for mothers keeps us young. Our feral spines become entwined in silken longitudes, lips like tiny hours aware of urgency those terrestrial habits changing certain fate. Working the pubis of earth with your hands, there was the near-death alarm or howl that illuminated the halls of purgatory. Its lime-green lights off then on was the picture of falling without end, nude pink lips of yesterday spoke a sort of bird warble they mentioned laconic bodies moving in dance or film, a coming-of-age narrative where we find ourselves, sensations of touch somehow become invisible mausoleums where we travel with death, a train track to commune with childhood: a reminder of suicide, those palpable details although you escaped most of all that, you sleep with the lights on not just night lights unless you have a "guest." I roll my "r's" waiting for the digital kiss of lips to suspend unaccounted for moments, the row of teeth on my tongue works out a course for shadowing words. Discreetly I mime a phonemic library between my lips: *Coño que bella*, a sulfur light buzzing on and off, bearing minuscule children of daylight, what was said was washed ashore to the endless chasms of rivers and lagoons where perched seagulls feast waiting for their daily bread, as I often do, when we look into the ghost twilight and moon kissed necks there are absent moments of silence filled with pale cigarette smoke, Adam without descendants in a motion sickness of years swaddling a figment of clay and god's breath.

Ancestral Dysmorphia

Your voice accentuating nimbus, thick gauze which were the earthen ghosts of ancestry. Syllables like cocoa or palm fruit having traveled from Baní, Dominican Republic to Nueva York. A half-opened page dedicated to descendants reading a prose poetry book of Jazz standards. Slipping obols into the change-purse of time. Two roads diverged like the tongue of an ouroboros swallowing itself and releasing what we already know. Karma feeds on those feeding on others which is something hard to swallow. Weary people housed within birdhouses remind the birds lyrics to their own songs like painted screens on a television set. There is a Cuban inside my ancestral dysmorphia like lost rivers finally finding their homes. Luz verde towering like aquamarine eyes oscillating like war from a lighthouse in my tiny body. Working on my hard skin of blues. There is a wall of umber enveloping my naked body traveling between rooms a storm of sand and dust where god watches in the calm waiting for more of its children to rise.

Oracle-Bloodline

The missionaries walked with blisters on their skin. Traveling the maze-like belly of the *finca*. They took a sliver of the scythe to the bowels of the field and exhumed its sugary cane. We were what was left. Next was grasping names from the villagers. A river that remembers each pair of passing feet plunged into its waters. Like a key with its cut filling the body of space. Some mistake prophecy for dreams where memory hangs like a ghost cashing food stamps; spending space money on what we all desire and then taxing the earth or blaming our friend for living and/or not doing so. A mass at an allotted time with god running marathons through a portal of a penumbra the size of a television screen. A conversation with amnesia on the navel of ash and dust, the thought of leaving familiar to longing. We spent the last days on neon orange steppes and the codex was written in indecipherable lines of the palm. There were the days passing like flocks of birds, messengers circling in tangents never quite coming to the pith of things. Someone thought you strange to wander in a land such as this working for your livelihood until the flesh unhooked from the bone. I saw how you were always peering into your vanity mirror as though it had scrying properties, hidden things were a mass of fleshy pulp as though Turkish *nóvelas* had some secrets to bestow. Sometimes the unnamable things can't be translated. In the green fields of passing time there was a silence that overtook the house and there like many times over my family walked as though spirits. Words like a thousand scripture within an alcove of years pondered the dark of an *apagón*. The way *la fe* had come and led us through family bloodline after bloodline. *Se fue la luz* they would say and off went the lights in *el campo*. We didn't see the hand trying to turn a page and give up. Moving from spirit world was as if a dreamlike travel to Colombia. As though we were bodies of Oracle-bloodline. The last breath of the dying let out Morse code to strange gods. And we let out wild wails like the veiled cry of Mary at the cross. Those last few minutes ran the perimeter of the eternal, and someone shut their eyes as though truth needed blindness.

Brevity

Having a finite amount of time on this planet
Bobbing a thread through a needle's eye
Mrs. Night waiting for the sedentary accounts of stars postulating death
Brevity can be a peck on the lips, a dirge for one's father
A sunbathing girl's kiss that followed you through the thighs of trains and pubis of secret gardens: the meaning of life sequestered in sea-green tide pools summoning us from our impatient brooding; like restive planets scrawling notations of travel
A spitting out of phosphorescent carnelian budding from the jaws of volcanos: eyes disrupting silence, a slow tangible reach into where the Canaanites took shelter
A chariot where god shook the heavens and earth, rattling in euphony;
Cages of clay and ichor
Mr. Sun sleepwalks past portraits of his past life
A clock motions to you, "over here."
You follow, your hair whiteness, body an arc of skin, you quickly turn away
Everything back as it was
What do you do?
A fate far worse than prior knowledge of events; changing nothing
One might say is egress to forgotten cities without name or being.

Ayer

In luminous talk between insomnia and work I found you plucking away at the ends of my books and old photos; salt cities bruised. Your warble-like cursive an odd anecdote, now; I am machine-migrant. Flight attendants gathering gossip, running back to fill a cup of coffee for my mother on her way home to Santo Domingo. Aghast with passing years; I was fifteen kissing nymphs. Family a gut of spirits, ping-ponging back and forth from a space of testimony. A port in a country where I've known the longing for poetry; a pilgrimage that casts the Arab west toward the sex of witches, not now but *ayer*

Intimations

Necessity is like the germinated bulb in isolation stowed away reading a book. We have seen the furrows of expression lines undress crossed bodies in anticipation of the rebirth of Christ. Clouds clasping over the sun like an egg white broach, moving keenly down a body of vermilion. The wax and wane of a dark-skinned body. I am smoking a cigarette waiting for life itself to detangle my hair and reconstruct the Harlem-Renaissance era before siesta. The water and Seagram's comes like a séance, a deluge of philosophy. Christening old memory with Julio Iglesias' charm, the vapor-like smoke leaving your lips as though a telenovela were scripting wild nothings in singsong.

Plainsong

Tiny elephants in a grove. Crooked gap-toothed river is a purification rite, clutching a fist-full of storm-silt to cook madness. A visitation of disorder slowly peeling itself off, rinds of restive cities declawed. A habit that started as a cigarette a day inflamed into Goya's witch; love is a rare unicorn found only in paintings of the renaissance era where it was befriended as sacrifice. A cooing growing into a steady roar, our sacrum a flicker of fire, as we postulate where rare horses have gone in and out of our lives, waiting for a gallop of white noise to blind us. Their music a plainsong we are still hearing all this time in their absence.

Pause

I have thought about what meaning to place in these gravitating thoughts, a fiery brocade of plumes whispering from a phoneline of wires. Meaning belonging to an appetite not so easily moored to the past. Wavy hills, lattices of opaque white, a small bluish lake bouncing back light from the sun. There's a space between lips governing the lapsing of life, a body struggling with mortality.
I think of the upturned leaves under my feet walking a trail in worlds lost to an age of information. We try to understand thoughts and words that spiral crookedly to an unknown destination. You may be the last to know. A dialect that crosses bordering towns. A relief to see you left parsing a language that a provincial farmland in a mountainous region could not abandon.

Eurydice

It is as though a mind wavering in a green gem of fog sees no further than the placid hand wandering the invisible. This in a kiss of bath rituals where ears pop, tiny terrestrial creatures high jumping from a bed comforter meeting your eyes with abandon. An inner lobe twisting, a backward e tracing the lining of the ear perhaps being kissed, a knowledge of an echo is sent reverberating down passed membranes we forgot belonged to us. A twang of a ferryman crossing the river Styx, where many have crossed its water's pinkish tinge, a brute gurgling noise consuming life. Navigating through darknesses collecting brightness. A whippoorwill trilling puffing its brocade of feathers. Light work by the hour where cantos are read by globes of fire. A well collects handsome fortunes in the silent world of dreaming. A plane flies by and a mallet slides along a singing bowl fishing for a ringing that never happens. Greeted atop a stairwell by a peck of light then a flood of saffron. As they ascended Orpheus looked back at his past finding nothing but shadow where Eurydice had stood. A singe of his heart was the thought in the pit of his bowels that he was alone having faced hell with only sadness as companionship.

Pyres

What if standing here hurried, weathering cloudbursts, a mute pause in the eye of the storm where we glanced up and saw a movie playing back our lives, sitting, rocking in a chair slowly, unfolding time waiting for what the few are granted, someone passed by and woke you from your spell of daydream, water pellets began to fall smearing make-up on the faces of strangers, you moved in your chair and saw your life, a river swallowing itself, tiny polished rocks shaped by your passing, skin moving over pools of water, suntanning by a collection of pockmarked faces, you saw the light scatter its olive skin between the folds of her neck, salsa dancing had begun to warm the ends of our bodies, running hands beneath the earth, building clay churches like pyres, what could it be? In this turbulent year we erected cities in a nightfall. Our limbs throbbing, we disappeared in the white dust.

Invisible Creatures

Lyre, a body of song, cowering from a strange dark
A promising gaze where Prometheus collected flint and kindling together and inflamed human history
When those years weighted by memories are your only children stirring ill befallen fate
A television buzzing white light in tandem with a stationary fan howling its plea to the moon-void
Neon alarm-clock glows with an aquamarine bite
A requiem for moments passing down the habits we keep
A plasticine siren calling for her Odysseus
A madman by the mast of the bed, wrapped in a comforter of white down
Juggling between the fingers of his hands a lotus fruit from which he inhaled and migrates to the far reaches of the sky
There is a beige woman pressing herself upon the hipbone asking me if I want something else
The body wanting nothing more than to turn all the lights out in the room and disrobe
To turn the shower on and wait for me
It's like being swept into the sea washing away black nightfall from unknown hands
Invisible creatures of earth's skin
A quickening like sterile eyesight those fragile egg membranes a crater of tiny birth
Where a bubble of sonic speed rubbed out the nib of nerve, warbling one to the other in hushed prose: mycelium like drums on an off-beat, oval shaped wombs with the hollow of estranged pitter patter of a phantom fetus, a river of tangents floating by like storms
We ship build this house a catacomb of *pandemia*

Blueish light at the traffic stop not knowing what to do
Your purse-shaped tongue that became hours of nude springs
Waters rage circulating through veins carrying chairs, Chevys and houses along with men, women, children and dogs chasing their tails like a carousel
A foreigner's words half here half there weighing a dimension of endlessness on what work means
A visitation of a passed father as my docile mind wanes over time moving away from us
Like milk herds gathering a flock into the silent gestation of night a silent ghost like popping a house would announce
Stillness measured in dark remedies
Dollops of quiet light

Abbreviated Space

(A) period of childhood traditions used to simulate time travel/ hardboiled and gasping for inner light some traffic of bruised fingers, knobby and waiting for change to swallow Jonah whole *along with a truckload of distractions. We would find him meditating on enumerable isolation, a (god), as night transpired within the whale's abdomen. We are all left weightless in this world confirming we all are a collection of thought matter and ash. Artful hands, lives scrawled into palms, light fingers wrestling with our fragile mortality. When Jonah was spit out of the sea (whale) where he had spent so much abbreviated space which was monstrous, there was a tiny light in the dark that flickered when it spoke.

Jazz Scriptures

"Reality is not always probable, or likely."   -Jorge Luis Borges

Populated cities, schools of phantoms dropping in through a peep hole wide as a chasm. Secret conversations we ease drop into from our bedroom, a quiet place where we lay onto a bed and sink deeper as though through the floorboard; there is no real time-space problem. A needle flicks over an imaginary record, a sound of its lapsing continues. Sometimes the heat of our stony bodies collapses onto itself, a domino of splendor. Veins on a bulging eye staring into a cistern. Waiting in a compressed room of invisible strings where a woman sings in a high-pitched voice as though children singing. The pacing had become a way to reenact a process being tended to in repetition that became performative. Houses floating above ours strung along by a silver umbilical-chord. A dabbing of weightlessness in a hull of a lit room. A traffic of flushed faces. Electrical currents passed through lobes of grey matter, there's a furnace of tangible thought. We spend days forgetting, pacing walls, a space tending to a colony of ghost-travel plucking arils off the skin.

Puja of Bodywork

A passing year on your bed lying under an arm of strange friendships pruning as an act of breath. Indian scents the solace of work. The resuscitation of things we sometimes take for granted; a foreign language translated by a sannyasi in broken eggshell teeth. There was a flight swallowing night, morning, and earth itself to Nepal. Where the mountains kept their kisses to the moon a public affair. Dayglow became sinewy treks up nameless mountains. Always *sadhana* working its gossamer on time. How much our course has changed? How mercurial Legba stands at the crossroad? To make a puja of bodywork, luminous cardamom skin. Sleep passes through the limbs of Vishnu. In the temples of Kathmandu summer rainfall fills watering holes and unreachable places in our bodies.

Fine Lines

Sometimes it gets to me: the lucid gnaw of azure night. The haunt is a long reminder of memory renewing its vows, nonplus phantoms collecting their things at dusk. Tedium reciting itself over again in this house. I would look down into my fingers and read the cryptic lines of chiromancy as though I could decipher stories of lives both lived and yet unknown.

Inertia

"If you want to know the past, look at your present. If you want to know the future, look at your present."

I hollowed my lips and my tongue patted the upper banks of the roof of my mouth making a talisman of qualms, I waited for the boat quivering back and forth; for the psalms of inquiry under duress. Painted nails an acrid litmus test of searching. Her hand was an exile of skin where an island ran between fingers translating broken language like fissures or hoops of yarn being tressed through with a needle. A palimpsest from a fond lover in history. A fog like milk-sky blindness. I struggled with the crumbling stone gaze walking backside front into the tarmac like a symphony performing in American Sign Language. There is a chance meeting one can expect to relish in the dusk of summer when all the birds have migrated to their abodes. Hands wavering like cities; hands maps to the otherworld. I thought about how much unspecified living had consumed us, its breath ionized sea air moving within us. Its betweenness are half-opened buds almost lips needling desire with a hoop of yarn crocheting a sweater to keep us warm for the winter.

"There is a place down there not grim with pain but only with sad shades whose deep laments sound not as screams but melancholy sighs."
 - *Dante Aligheiri*

New Mythology

For Jarvis Jay Masters

Tiny hands in a locked cell, light pronounces from new things like a desert of spherical diurnal heat. An eggshell dome of peaceful breath ruminating on sitting time, its ponderable essence placated by weighted thoughts passing into paired hands clasped together in sacred communion. Throaty words pitchy and olive-like sent pausing trimesters of perilous creatures down the backs of arms, tiny hairs searing centuries of vast wastelands. There is something in the mist of ionized rest livid with ghosts parting with life still alive. Days upended waning watching as hours pass, lucid moments, and past mistakes the intervals of thoughts passing by careening as though silent ships would appear in a sacred dance. They blindfold madness and name the stars after Greek mythology, those foreboding tragedies shadowing life itself. A screen with a projector of shadowy images racing up and down the backs of incarnadine skies. Our bodies being released into the atmosphere phantoms of memory.

Amnesiacs on a Schedule

I think of what really could happen to the time spent thinking of strangers in bed. The books being read cover to cover with haste. Trains cascade by like amnesiacs on a schedule. Letting the hollow of tablas ring for eons in a kirtan. Humid air trapped in a second story bedroom. The glare of paranoia penetrating each pupil. Rooms that could be heard from every layer of skin on my body. Words that tell god I have another secret for you. The lavender night caws like a crow.

Hard Candy

We bear certain signs, a perennial light. You mull over the static that hinders our stars, that dysmorphic tarrying from a peripheral short sightedness. An old angst strong arming a tiny jetty as strangers whisper and talk, cold and incarnadine, their casual lives away against a blue reflection of television neon. Its incalculable calm washing away, a ripe tide-like snare. You worship time- its exhausting breath bee lining from your lips, hard candy. A parting of clouds or seas. A train collapsed in a traffic of pleasure that odd hum in sync with a palpable kiss of exhumed memory. A vertigo of accident where Jazz records are handed down to foreign fingers in velvet rooms. Dry kiss/ storytelling over skin where sleeping angels read the liner notes from parsed madness: day glow someone reach the sky/ see egg whites running out of time/ low key reason bet you would not mind/ try to tell me what you really want to find.

I was there standing against a wall smoking a cigarette wishing I never smoked at all although I was happy I had something to do with my hands. I felt there was something ethereal about that night the way you placed your hands on mine. Soft silk carrying me down through hard lines. She nodded and asked if she knew me from a dream she had; I wondered if she was joking or slightly off. After she took me away someone from the band walked up and reminded her, she had a show to play. The set was incendiary, and I wondered how I could live such a life the high of the performance was such a rush. One day I will write a novel about going to concerts and having and not having that kind of love.

In spaces of dizzy heat the silences between what we are and what we are becoming hourly peering into the cosmos. Thick, black vertigo, a passenger train pacing back and forth chasing little nimbus clouds of heaven stopping at every bardo to rain down its touch of amber skin. We touched god's hands under tables whispering our regrets and noble pursuits. She told me to answer the phone with a ringer that sounded like the Velvet Underground. Someone's Jazz ran down my dark arm those sweet votive songs lifting my tiny hairs almost like a snake rattle or tambourine murmuring to madness. I am nowhere. Sitting here reading, watching the lines cascade by thinking about who I am becoming. It is like Jazz all these strange thoughts, a cacophony of memory or a dissonance of strange angels. Waiting for a new mythology to migrate through my body.

Juggling

Sitting under a tangerine spotlight analyzing dreams remaining somewhat aloof you begin to question anima permeating through pinholes of creative longing. A kingdom of white heat drawing a line between art and artist creating out of a list of necessities. Whereas life recreates death without dying via a synthetic womb. An abridged life lived on stage in several acts where tragedy is communal. Ribbons of arrows touching modern skin, unearthing a world on fire. It was heaven-like those years spent fascinated by a glowing mist telling us we were hybrid bodies. A diurnal trance had us slipping coins into a clothes dryer watching as we began to slowly age. Years passing quietly, rhapsodic immaturity being slowly cooked-to-ready/ an egg timer tentatively prodding us to line bookshelves with (un)approachable beauty/ a handsome future pulled from a ubiquitous fortune cookie you saved and made your own/ careful with how you juggle lapsing time.

Earworm

Earmarked thoughts launch a drove of specters
Banging, plying hands, ghost fingers looming in space
Talk between trains ferments in the snow cast muted night
What are words but passengers between cars that know each other's lips
Dutiful strange entities working the nib, an earworm digging into silence

Childlike

For Jackie

Resin seeping into a bay of earthen sleep at the center of words a knuckled fist, a ball of kiss. Rhythmic eyes tensing a timing like seismic craters. A coma that took place in the terminally afraid places of rainfall, a place that followed us, a family over lifetimes. A television watches your last conversation with me, those final words and a firm hug searching for your future life at a college that never happened. They say you were going to be a pediatrician, your shaved head, convulsions wondering when things can be the same as before. You died the same year as my dad, and I am left wondering what that means. I think of chance meetings governing life, its bird odyssey committing to strange words. We are here peering down into the sitting area of god's throne room mingling with his favorite angels and somehow, I see you borrowing a book or two as you were wont to do here on earth in this house and I watch your smile and wait for the words of god to say take another my child.

Code-Switch

We use symbolz for our commonplace phenomena.
Layers removed from what is found within arms-length.
Awe-struck by how language is a code being broken between interminable people. A gathering in what seems like forests as well as androgynous co-living spaces where family and friends resurface to commemorate newly amended words in the Oxford-Dictionary: code-switching between identifying language and oral history that crashes on forgotten islandz.

Tiny Parakeet

Its sinewy breath thin cirrus clouds of sapphire
A church parking lot condensed with dress hats and fur lined coats
A tiny mass of candles in a parking lot for a dead twenty-year-older lined with empty rum bottles
I remember when he was alive passing me by on the block with a very friendly and pretty white girl with a fuchsia peacock tattoo-
And he was telling me how we should practice our *don* or make a schedule of pursuing what dreams are: in the colliery world of unearthing what we will one day become
Sometimes without reason a tiny parakeet dies from song not from carbon monoxide poisoning
Then we can see god willfully shows others how living beautifully is a beauty in and of itself and the cost is not death but living happily in another life somewhere in god's diorama, perhaps

Lifecycle of Stars

Sometimes it hits like ephemera or a plane colliding with the earth/ The craziness like raw yolk running down my hair// *Que locura*// That silent pulse reverberates down my spine when we touch/ Your soft laugh like fingers looking for skin/ I am wondering about the surface of the earth and its cilia captivating the birdsong/ I have imagined the echo of your face moving towards me like the slow gestures of a plastic bag eschewed by the wind/ I sat contemplating your anecdotes as we ashed into cut open Coca-Cola cans filled with water/ Filling what life had allotted us into slivers of changing seasons like the lifecycle of stars sending phonetic messages from space like the tappings of a merengue drum solo/ Dreams where we speak to each other in a foreign language and are still understood like a sea that meets a collection of unnamed rivers/ There are quiet lips relegated for other lips waiting for the proper moments/ I have thought about the philosophy of isolation/ The seduction of expectation; its vibrato/ Then relinquish the idea of it, the affirmation of love left pending for unnamed *locura*.

Light Work

Moving through a flickering of ghost shadow, hounded by history. Night sweat on an upper lip. Let down without much provocation, the cataract surfacing like short tempered argonauts. A universe speaks its native language to astral cities in space. Life has its qualities contained in nakedness, darknesses, light matter, youthful exuberance, and patience; being inherently good: a sonogram reading a poem of birth, pockmarks on cheeks from years as a teenager, waiting to cohabitate with friends or lovers. Synapses longing to be understood and felt, the realization that we have all been hurt too. Yet we move on, a slow drift of earth cascading down to our naked feet.

Stars and/or Gods

"The word 'song' is used to describe the pattern of regular and predictable sounds made by some species of whales"   -*Wikipedia*

Cerulean sky: nocturnal sonar singsong, schools of sienna or a disorder like Jazz, a silk reed saturated in cool sweat. I marked my arms with fine lines an homage to graffiti art from New York City and/or Paris. Somehow my body was a silent ode to children's drawings despite being legitimately able to draw. The wax poetic of an allegory of unrequited love like a reciting of elegies to stars and/or gods. Those who have a habit of waking up late into the evening are left feeling as though the warning lights have been lit and there are ominous forces letting us know we do not have much time left. At one time I lit a cigarette that lasted from one afternoon until nightfall, those are the perks of *magical realism*. To be awakened to the three forms of time: past, present, and future some mystics concluded would end in liberation. An organ player talked to himself between the bars his feral hands went livid like a neon clock that marked time correctly twice a day we concluded: "song."

Driving Blind

Hypnotic roads disappearing, a vanishing point merging with strobing headlights, a sky fire. We egg on unrecognizable patterns keeping us awake in a balm of night. A bog of misshapen thoughts, passing by in jerky flushed strokes. Near-death brushes with fate engorging capillaries, a surge of ruby-red stained cheeks. When we close our eyes to breathe for a split second it is a hyphenated moment in time before more asphalt. Keeping an eye on the meridian we make our own nascent notions of rising from a ghost train. Warm-blooded digits gripping a steering wheel until the palms are pale. A distant sound of kirtan on the radio and my jowls howl a red song. A hollow of darknesses, a blue movie where we unclothe and steadily watch with lucent eyes as though nocturnal animals.

Saffron-touch

Pondering the contents of an oracle trance, where peculiar worlds are a science of familiar people speaking through golden wires, saffron synesthesia, word for word, a collection of dust-mites, gathering flame. Habits of extended silences with conversations amongst the neon-void, invisible voices: silent rumination, a pattering of geese flight, the crease of origami paper flecked with green eyes. Winnowing down the corridor shuffling by the past selves of our lives, a sore wound being plied open to siphon the splinter of childhood.

Sapphire Clouds

Those weblike fingers scrawling, orbiting terrestrial skin. Tiny fractals of light. A red sun revealing ominous ghosts in the room. There was something alarming about the weighty mind-stuff cross-pollinating with a foreign tongue lining the cheeks, straying into the unknown of taciturnity, a Möbius strip of travel. Reasoning with a rattle of thought, little pulsing diodes of peach and aquamarine light, an indecipherable chicken warble as though its anguish was headless, gasping for air and/or taking its last breath; slowly filling with sapphire dust. There is a second-floor balcony collecting the pockmark of cigarette pale heat and the nuanced travel of thought. A forest of spiraling lines has led to foreign lands their oblong arc watching you from a perilous height, viewing you from a pinpoint of a future courted by blindness. The daylight of Jazz was a séance: a summoning, a shadowboxing, vermilion hip-talk, and folk-whispers in odd hours of wakefulness. It takes a while to process the fast blip of singsong, the Caribbean Sea-salt accumulating on my body. The lapse of moving frames watching from a window jetting by inside the Metro-North train. A space between my lips condensed to hold you, say this is real, and exhume sapphire clouds. A pink nipple jutting out from an areola the size of a silver-dollar revealing itself like a tiny windfall of nude heaven. A euphony of distances being met. Something foreign that you recognize as familiar, a samskara from a childbirth of lives prior. The ache of Jazz. Its testimony baptizing the earth.

Sepia Light

Film like a finely toothed comb wailing back and forth throughout history without memory. The words are left imprinted, a disappearance is some strange afterglow wrestling with the construct of nations. The borders fitting themselves between the thighs of passersby, an allusion to Christ's passing somewhere in Arabia. What could the mysterious sigils of yesteryear have to say about us? I sat watching a coronation of Solomon from centuries past and overheard an exchange of whisperings between him and god. As the cars float by and ambulance sirens breathe in the warm night air. I have been talking to you waiting for the last line to write itself taking perilous drags from my cigarette. There was the thought that god too had a child. The next day became a year and half later leaving me long lists of questioning. The bruise on your thigh, clove skin and olive fingers: collecting the memory of people moving through lit windows, wires of light, or fuchsia lightning storms. This sepia became an ashtray where I finished my naked tasks. A light stray and choppy giving one the impression of growing (four) arms from your torso to help you with difficult tasks. A pulpy blur of thought treading water at a desk.

Feral Headlights

I finally caved into your touch. Your slow breath calming the lights of a town. The feral headlights passing by are livid planets, a hoary minotaur swallowing a golden thread tracing history, youth; a blue god staring at himself in a mirror of your soul. They let the darkness become a blind spot, a glaucoma. The red flames of questioning. It takes me to an unrecognized cemetery. Where I walk around and plumb a bitch-brew. I am sitting beside you as you unfold time before me.

Nude Gem

Frenetic, a shadow tour in a room breathing, pulsating, and working in tandem. A revelation, the last book a plexiglass window where we look straight through into some familiar person, we are fixated on their nude body ambling in space. This stasis, those nuances of desire plumbing vacated alcoves, a small volume of words burgeoning from an abdomen. Thought matter condensed like tiny star diodes popping in and out of existence, an echo chamber like strange hands of isolation built within walls. A new sun growing feral, stray dogs in heat chasing each other round. Livid bodies. This is Villa Juana where bachata plays in hidden alcoves reminding people they had lovers once; when I was too young to know love but old enough to desire it. Strange madness began to singe my skin, hours on the phone twirling the phone cord wrapping it round my finger until it finally unhooked from the line. At what decibel are these people hearing our thoughts in a planetary Jazz. Breath tightening, asphyxiating in a tiny desert lodged within the rim of our lungs, our bodies quiet songs lapping up silent birds tweeting a missing miracle. A vocation of flight this nude gem, an ancient recourse of unfathomable dissonance.

Glow

Someone gets these nerve endings to speak again, silent parties where we sit down and share parts of our bodies, lives, skin, skinny folds wrapping around fingers. Sometimes not knowing becomes a church where you sit and pray inside the pews. Folds of skin waiting for more congestion. Hours later watching as people file out feeling relieved as if they have become someone else all this time unaware of themselves fumbling, tiny hands knocking on their brains, "let me in," and "let me out," waves of this flood us until we walk home. Not knowing who we are, unaware of where these thought-whispers have arisen in this Lazarus-like afterlife. Onlookers watch from the foyer the legs of passersby. What has this wind swept into our bodies? A disorder where you call sentences into rooms and let them ferment, they radiate like ionized, jagged asterisks where they are mentioned * grief, loneliness, despair, anxiety, psychosis, paranoia, alienation, weight loss/weight gain, stress, etc. There in tiny places our hands throb like ghosts writing novels about their past lives. Grief lines of a pandemic: we often fixate on the irretrievable, its brute force a vanishing line. To wander in a spellbinding delusion: oblivious of reality, sleepwalking in a fog of loneliness, pangs of ephemeral highs and lows like waves. I have noticed the teetering of an oscillating fan washing away a traffic of silence, a mythology of life. The storytelling of diurnal gods. A bed of memory where a strange guardian walks their rounds. Lit windows a germination of lives evolving from tiny seeds. We meet strange angels on a grocery line, on our way to work, while we chat with old friends, sometimes we talk with one of them our lives tiny bulbs unfurling.

Hopscotch

Ash and dust collected on the tongue of the ashtray, loneliness like a gaze in trepidation awkwardly floating away never to meet the follicles or ends of your eyes as they are the ravines reserved for people cast aside bearing tiny hubris for that unwelcomeness. Building stony factories of incandescence with the irksome weight of abandoning homeland and namesake. Grief swelled the lips of the sucking bird as she nursed agony despondently like a trucker gleaning the road daydreaming of family. Stories that bruise, a brute familiar daze ripening in the recourse of a gesture, wordless like a fortress in a Dominican heat with those sienna-skinned women and men like carnal folkloric apparition dancing that invisible dance: invisible to the tourist, the megalomaniac. With a trancelike hopscotch like a sheath over the old pueblo, its timbre speaks to the traveler in a Haitian accent selling *maní*, women *en luto* dressed in black like death refused to hear the musicians, their spiral of heaven.

Cinema

Somewhere in between the two lines a firing ground. An axis of earth spiraling into silence. Those missing teeth pulled from adolescence kept for posterity's sake. I spent the night plumbing the ichor seas: god's bloodline, milk, or amrita. Watching its pulse rise and fall on the hour. Its heft like the weight of angels. Words around hips or across lips like ephemera ducats we use for a lifetime that will not carry us into any celestial places. I was rummaging through the dog-eared moments of my past life which made me brusquely nod off into the afterlife. As I imagine the near dying do with their glassy eyes of contemplation rocking back and forth in time barely moving. A sort of ghost travel through towns and cities where we meet our strangers and lovers over and over again like a row of dice sent into oblivion with its incestuous faces. Reworking history in our brief life its snake-like song uncoiling like a catacomb of forgotten libraries. There is not much of a guarantee in this experience we call life. Its granular accommodation of living and dying. We can see time as a beige or pastel wall, and we are the painters exhausting the supply of paint. In another life we could go to a store and buy forest-green paint and continue another wall somewhat like the wall we were painting. Some say the self always paints the wall and the memory of painting it always exists. Some say that we are here to paint a forest of walls in a collective mansion. I might say it is not just paint. I collect my things and wonder at the rarity of life. The analogy of past lives and meaning of life which remain brief and vague. I take a drag from a cigarette and wonder this time how brief? Its syncopated breath tressed with Jazz and nude terrestrial fires. In the sapphire heat of earth naked in a lagoon where the youths couple up and find a place to grow old together. Its half-light like crimson-enameled teeth. Singing along to madness. Its sensibility like the rattlesnake's row of inner teeth swallowing the world itself. The passing by of time like mute phonetic gestures of hands-on bare stomachs watching the tiny hairs glisten like peach lightning. There are gods in a silent peck, an overcast kiss, burnt ochre misspellings waiting for signs in Jazz, aquamarine brothers and sisters, half pear-shaped bodies wrapped in other bodies. The weight of touch turning on its axis pushing itself eternally up a hill, upward and back like the body in its own trajectory. The buzz of homeostasis like the pull of want measured in small increments calling on a need to its highs then lows like a reminder we are all children of our own devices. The needle and the thorn. Its hapless kiss turned tentacle arm to take a drag of sea-green smoke. The wish for the same greedy puff is helpless. We walk the past up the hill tirelessly until it reaches the bottom again. Sisyphus is mentioned in memory then forgetting his name and place of birth. Satiated by the process of search but not enough to quit the act entirely. Its endless loop a wildfire of reciprocity. Sometimes ruminating on the consciousness of forget, longings remind us it is still raining tiny blessings. I noticed you somewhere in a collection of thoughts that kept me from moving from house to house like a song that refuses to stop playing. As though Jazz were calling me from a different room its beige hum like a visitation. Waiting to number the walls filled with a snow-white horned Minotaur as I remembered the sort of offhand commentary that life is like a sepia film. When that horned bull arrived, I accommodated him by the couch with the frills, peanut butter chocolate, Coca Cola, and popcorn. We were watching the story of my life, weren't we? It went dark and I will not ruin the ending for you, not this time.

PDA like the Half-life of a Plum

I have been left grappling with the kissing and shoulder meetings/ those uncomfortable pitfalls where strangers visit each other's cheeks and fig-like lips/ Public display of affection an acronym// PDA// a resonance like flirtatious buzzing that germinates within the solemn walls of fingers// in churches// where they come en masse an opacity of spirit/ In conversation with the past like a continuum of incarnations where we have convinced ourselves that the pithy gestating sienna hands over mulatto skin is a celestial place for making soft incises into amrita/ the nature of emptiness its aquatic membranes were unexamined like a dream of gods where we fashion our livelihood/ a coupling of breath and senses satiated perhaps by prayer/ absent like stifling pulpy pecks/ to rise and erupt from a pew/ watchful of the uninhibited collapsing over a tiny Latina woman with a wonder that leaves the fumes of a burning kettle its twangy pangs as though someone had removed its stopper; a siren of attraction/ I sit and watch the strands of hair swallowing nude skin like a witness to the indecipherable minutiae between the bruise of unseen lips// pulpy, thin fingers// I wait calmly until I can talk to you again/ a brusque nod to a far off point in time when you were still here and I could hear you say sort of facetiously that you were proud of me/ in the mass during the day of the dead with the intention to remember you I find myself wondering what strange motif has circulated amongst the hour while the past and what has become of the present arises/ The jade neon brings strangers home an unaccounted for plus one and allows us to nominate most likely to run away from history at our past life reunion.

Night Vision

It has been a while since I have spoken to you. A nocturnal scent of otherness. The sound of the radiator comes in. A cigarette waiting to bloom amber. I waited for words to finish with a whiplash. We live in consent to fall at the feet of gods. Praying with inoculated lips. What does the author read of disjointed sutra? Mystic oblation and the rest of the day contemplating whether life is real or illusory. The friends waiting for me, my family and even this old town. Could we be an old pueblo in a haunting where Pedro Paramo like Adam is father to all of us ghosts? I look out of my window and ruminate over the meaning of existence. Schizophrenia is a fawn drinking from a silver lake of mercury, cupping her last messages of ancestry. Language of memory and reality no different than a dialect of foals huffing. Driving around town listening to early Jazz, I mistake nodding off into a dream as jargon for god-teeth. Cursed fingers letting go; we sat in the park talking about places that were distant and foreign. I still go on about desire on lips and touch easing itself into wanting. An opium of your skin on mine the difference of dialect, two passenger trains in Calcutta emptying themselves. A helix of what was lost. Hearing the fire escape in deep longing, I waited for the exhumed sigh of hungering. A cloudburst and a phone's numb pomp going in and out of service. Lying here with the windows reflecting the room, a proverb where she does not forget me after she walks away is new mythology.

"Now I am become death, the destroyer of worlds"
 -*Krishna*

Anthology of Ancient Anxieties

"A style is a means of insisting on something"   -*Susan Sontag*

Plasticine growth akin to eating wisteria or oleander. A mouthful of toxins. Attributed to the tiny pitfalls of November. Candidates weathering the last dance. This talk show host baffled by green screen, a quixotic questionnaire. A blank ballot with miscellaneous misspent youth somewhere below. A fictionalized account of certain events in history. Nothing out of the ordinary. Insistence is prolific rainfall in spring, a tiny Porcelain doll pirouetting; amassing great weight: an anthology of ancient anxieties, downcast fuchsia eyelids and the thick magenta of heartache crashing on a stranger's couch. Strange bedfellows are crimson hands stained with dust reading those obscure spiraling(s) of fingerprints while caressing the second moon of the terrestrial planets. On and on the humming of birds, eggshell flight, its hybrid twang. Somniphobia: I have developed a sleep anxiety, the thought of loss, its arcing arms fixated on the digital clock on my phone, the rise and fall of empires, my sienna chest that shudders away from no death.

Rivers of Elysium

Terminals of passenger trains are jilted angels, saccharine olive fingers, dove-like the modality of insistence beating ominously upon a velvet radio that hums Velouria at strange timbre, chasing that radical tinge of tobacco that sweetens and brazens with an astringent shriek of lonesome cloud-breath, the eyes madden and daze to kiss the folds of celestial abodes, we were not strangers to the dark places that led us like dancing grave-diggers unearthing the holes to unspeakable wombs, tiny transistors that were walkie-talkies not of this realm, we placed the hand upon books, scrolls of Vedas unrolled to let their luster bear itself more like a manifold etching of pilgrims, the work decided to half feed their bodies with simulacrum, and we took our final guppy breaths over and over until we exhausted night and Chandra began to give us questioning looks with his eye for the consistency of our perilous doldrums, years and years like iron being put to rust we became a modicum of strange hands plying sadhana from our dry lips, gasping soft in undulating moans like the teat of the witching hour, so much time spent plowing the fields of Elysium with rivers of lucent eyes, cities deafened and we knew no sound, the clawing of the clucking crow were the ill portents of omens everywhere, still pressing on as though Lazarus were reincarnated from the dead as a Lama, the dead speak in parables with tongues decorated with eyes, auburn hair in the teeth like a perdition, she couldn't count all her blessings in a collection of decades as they kept amassing weight like clasped irons and gravity, the enamel became a curse for the song on my lips, a honey tasting of cherub candy suffice to say the flavor was sweet ambrosia and there was nothing like it to compare, I've waited years or was it I've prepared the night to cauterize the fleshy duppys in the absence of this citadel, some see the church as a spire likened to babel that was saved by god and they're still wandering in this cacophony hanging in the rafters of those missing attics of sadness, I've no indecent comment to make of the debate between those missing teeth of conformity ranging in the apex of nuance like a hipbone shipbuilding hangers-on by the flick of the wrist without purpose, haplessly revoking the spirit and the red card like flannel in a missing letter never sent almost as if on purpose but we all know much better than that.

Catacombs

Planetary oval lights transmigrating through pools of ether.
Ash domes, a whippoorwill trilling. There in an unpacked
room a millennium of stars passengers of bluish light. A nod of
opaque sapphire where autonomous creatures smirk and tread
through memories. A child's grizzly laugh as though pleased with
circumstance auspiciously placed in their laps. There is seldom a
reason to think people in passenger trains or passing strangers
have not lived such an easy life as the one you are living. Cars
tressed with Indian food, a kiss on the hip then to the pocket
of skin near the stomach and elsewhere, a travel around towns
where you collect names: beads of amethyst or amnesia, waking
or sleeping, wandering or idle, a tidal wave between the legs may
bring a foreboding transit of books from one shelf to another,
a slow escape of indescribable words; they sleepwalk along
catacombs. At bedtime hands unclasp and mirrors are sapped of
their own music, a furnace of books collecting heat: wise words
rise from rosy lips saturated with cold sweat. But this was the end
as well as what you mentioned of a beginning in passing.

Island of Tangents

As dusk persuades us to come to terms with an abrupt distancing: the planetary half-light; neon fuses lodge into space. It is a never-ending loop of youth. Those unending elastic rivers measuring volcanic kisses, menstruating hands, dilated wombs giving birth to insomniac gods and goddesses. Each pale cigarette a layer of time raining down, unfolding over copper fingers laced with lapsing breath. There is a well slowly filling with a substance that remembers us: our past lives with women we have loved, an island of tangents, hair curled by sea air, mother and father, a brother, and cousins. It seems she does not care for what I do, the looking on as if I had not just said a few words of consequence. I wonder if though it was a well filling until it overflows. What could become of these days becoming more days as I keep adding to the well of reminders? Now a grayed-out reflection waiting to become clearer. When we see what we have come to see there is still the pleasure of living a life, of enjoying what we have sown.

Pedro Páramo's Phantoms

Jesus Palacio 1930-2020

A vertigo of sutra that became a collection of birds. Read over and over like an echo. We see our ephemeral passage milkweed bodies of the clutch. An artifact of a puja rising like cloud cities. Twilight carrying our desires to a place where future sans names are only the warbling of the universe. To consider staying here in this labyrinth, putting on a meter and taxying god. The question remains whether it is like staying in a town of phantoms. Pedro Páramo reading his astrology, his father walking through walls; a dust of stars.

Strange Bats

Dilapidated room, lights off, windows in full bloom
Falling into a pear shaped pitcher, socializing or lack thereof; feels like drowning
All this conversation takes place in the sitting room of my mind, take a seat, grab yourself something to read while we (I) negotiate terms.
Yes, it's the same poem
Only
The format is thinner
Cerulean pomp given Zeus' progeny would burst out from the skull with the slightest headache
Sheen collecting hoary doting looks patting yourself on the back
Dissolving muted talk in the region of the brain where patterns pitter patter silently like house cats
Tracing their ancestry back to its feral counterpart they purr and hunt odd thoughts into a database collection: wordsmith, poetry, books, voyeur, recluse
shorelines of wires, screen-to-screen, visceral non sequential habitual schizophrenia
I worry and wait for reason to marry my friends away
These life partners are long distance healing sessions
Strange bats are colossus driving to work late not caring if anyone notices but afraid of losing the only job I have ever really (   ) enough to care about; simple pleasures
A balm of sleep, smoking a cigarette halfway to the nib
A ring of halos around nude fingers
Sleep rings underneath your eyes

Catalog

After Yusef Komunyakaa

We are strange creatures walking nocturnal streets, waiting for first signs of bluish light. Brushing off near catastrophe, run ins with late peril, quirks a reanimating lit screen, dodgy motion-graphics foreshadowing solitary moments: emotions of longing, a repetitive pang of searching beyond oneself past unmistakable boundaries, leaving teeth marks on your tears as they shed in surrealistic paintings, letting your friends leave you in abandoned towns, being swallowed by a monstrous whale where we become so self-involved; we wonder how Jonah found god in a place like that. A moon orb, wobbly light pacing back and forth tethered to pink clouds as the drive through snaking roads is a rain dance. If we would begin to name each of the heaven's stars starting from the very first emanation, continuing in passing lives, until we have cataloged occult kingdoms, there would be a legacy of lives filled with mouths for no other purpose but for identifying and labeling a neon vernacular. We would be a fuzzy connection affixed to rabbit ear antenna for those watching from a distant future from some other dimension in time-space. By the time, all the long history of naming was ever even half complete. An index of red flames burning pinhole like dots measurable by how fast light travels. Then the ancient waiting game where we wind-up a jack-in-a-box and, "pop," everything is meaningless, and you cannot take anything serious anymore. To only laugh at god's sublime jokes and without qualms reserve yourself to the places you have been invited. To sleep all night with your eyes open, dreaming of sleeplessness. Fizzles of rain from a town of passing clouds where we wrestle with the bebop of ghosts.

Mecca

A small flood swallowing breath
Peering into each other's eyes wondering history, passing thoughts questioning worth
Ants on the dish have scouted a last Mecca of sweetness
Light in a room, we harbor its effusions, a pinpoint of explosion encapsulated in space
Where thought wanders freely on an open palm searching for warmth over a flame
Rubbing skin together, searching over mounds and dunes
Jumping from one questioning thought to the next
Failing to capture pithy rest in the nook of desire
Another one-sided conversation about your life
Gasping for air after so and so had smoked the last cigarettes (you)
Weight gain/ weight loss/ weight gain
Endless texts to people you never see
It's as though they are imagined or video simulation(s)

Indigo Village

Hours fade saturated, heady eyelids
It is this old town feeding a hungering
Watchful of passing light leaving you alert and buzzed
Tenuously sitting beneath a glowing sun
Fistfuls of satisfied days, heavenly bodies dregs of pale heat,
We walk home tentatively breath to breath
Where you happen to lay longer than memory
We see motion pictures carried to the queen of the colony
Beside the deck in neon skin bathing in a whirling well of indigo
breath, a gaping asterisk.
A row of windows peeking outward, an intoxicating night
A peach glow in a room of vibrating hands
Parsing meaning from a pool of unclenched fists
Bathing in a river of it as though we could reach the tips of the shore
Mouths were omens of nearby places accepting love,
a diary of travel
Half-open palms being read, a moon-pearl between teeth,
kissed by a probing tongue
A village of pale neon where the libraries are farmland
A dream catcher by the headboard as passenger trains outside loop
in and out of existence,
A heavy flame sending us to places in the dark without rest
An undressing of habits, a pause for silken thoughts to pass by like
flitting trains
As though we were to be reminded of events that stay new to us
We wake up and put clothes on our bodies
There is the thought that we may exist in someone else's life
unlike how we picture ourselves now.

Phylum of Jazz

"Always listen for what you can leave out."   -*Miles Davis*

I notice you say things beyond language. Sometimes memory peeks back at me reading a book or smoking a filtered cigarette wondering when any of this will make sense. Late at night I watch myself unravel the phylum of Jazz notes. In the convoluted night club of my mind, I lie in bed listening to records wondering what god is really trying to tell me beneath the apex of immeasurable stars. As another *greca* of coffee is made, I am left thinking how I can compete with the silence of these months. Those luminary windows that tell their own stories. Perhaps, god came to Isaac in such a manner. The story where Jazz became like words and the fecund madness was our religion.

Mulatto Colony

It permits travel down the god trail into absentia there in the city of the world between your amber thighs. I have been lighting this eternal cigarette with a brass flip open lighter watching the bed contort between breaths. The numbering of jasper beads between the syllable of fingers. I have been talking to the stars' turquoise, its jet lagged messages come in waves like sky fire. Short brutal oceans docking at strange lands, a new colony of humanity. My dark skin like intangible nimbus moving towards the pale fire. Sitting in a colonnade of an old Spanish city, on an island with the scent of sea salt and rum. I wander questioning the Braille teeth of the streets whether we are communicating one to the other. I consider the ethos of Santo Domingo its lit votive *velas* to Haiti, Africa, and Spain. Some forget an unconscious act the nuances of trying to retrieve something removed from our consciousness as blindness. We read it on our hands the fine lines working itself into unresolved future. Our mothers reading the minuteness of travel where borderlands kiss softly mulatto men and women.

Isolation

"I tried to feel the untitled thing that blossoms in me."
                                                    -Jorie Graham

Tiny woodland creatures scurrying into their homes. Retelling our stories over decades as though ghosts moved through us and animated our silken skins. What was left of the emptiness after we wet our lips with azurite and chaos connected our abbreviated silence? A howl that was the submerged vacuum of space one would call isolation slowly growing within a red chest like a mountain of indifference. The books being read collected in a room touching clouds in cerulean skies. This sad immutable sun, a TV set sits immobile, high to the east with a traffic of guffaws and neon wit. Pockets of smoke carrying stray dogs back to a netherworld of paralysis. Walking in circles around tiny planets. A figment of your voice populating my skin, pursing its contours. An unreliable flickering darkness. Straggling orbs of light appear/disappear like diodes from some other galaxy doing busywork or bulbs of lotus-feet blossoming with each ominous step.

Escaping

This may be an escaping, planting body on hands. Peeking in and out of eternity, spending choir money on elusive dreams, spaces in between muteness, those first tentative steps forward (e) with punch-drunk candor, walk/ running in step with a drum machine. In an insurmountable act of bravery, or something akin to fear (e), mulling it over, its gravity a quirk of patience. As voices from the heart thump their way through/ out. Brief episodes of sequential disorder: being set aflame, add sucking marrow from bone, (e), a morning sliding through my fingers, not knowing what comes next. A Metro-North train half here, half already in the otherworld clacking by its sonorous machine limbs chasing a currency of (e), there in a warbling light, plotting destination back and forth/ people gathering weight a kaleidoscope of great mass this tumbleweed of living moving along a flatland/ prairie. Only to relinquish our baggage: its thoughts, those ideas, or ideals, our history, we would let go of our bodies, amber hands, our olive lives performing for each other while we should be working. (e)

* escaping

Scriptwriter

Day's sweat is a brusque ending/ arid, accumulating like black dust in a blue flame/ Cities muted with satellites, the weight of hands on a pulse/ Questioning thought matter, sprawled over tangled Sargasso, nude ripe hours, a searching/ Pinions of ochre birds moving in flight/ A field of dust/ Grooming our former lives in future/ Grafting weight, ionized skin, un-slumped shoulders, above all else untangling gossamer that fits like a spiderweb of caves to finite places where celestial realms have made a certain possibility of us/ A fingerprint: tactile, we meet the synthesis of touch, a knowledge of kissing, its passage through bodily forms, a conversation of how earth grows within form, oblivion follows a pathway of sinewy skin/ A temple of thought-clouds peering into a spiraling palm some mention a script written by gods: we may read promise, forget, school children gathering rain, long years of marriage or an island of *magical realism*, we may only see what we are, it's an accumulation of windfall leaving you questioning what could go wrong.

Hazel Heat

Wirings restrung lopsided like the age of loss, tilting in half-neon. We could somehow wrestle with purpose flecked with olive light. Long days a talisman of selfhood or hot vernacular: cherishing thoughts, specks blown off nightstands, tiny infinite space being thrown into gravity, crashing into a shaft of mind-stuff where a pool collects the residue of quiet heat. A streetlight running its course, the prickly warmth of a woman's touch. Half-open buds, a meeting ground for opal-headed boys and girls. Whether we see light in the sky or have to dig the earth like urchins, a half-light surrenders to us all. Between the knobby knees of adolescence squinting our eyes into the sun. We gather our bodies, they are parks where we undress and become nameless. Navigating through invisible dreams. Womanhood like a flame of hazel heat hip-talking you through your vision quest. Wearing down your skin, the lining under your eyes and any chances you will ever have. Thoughts between travel; you begin to pick up loose reminders as though you have dropped them off at the laundromat. A wondrous walk with a collection of hands and arms, moving over you as though they were innumerable, like a Hindu goddess. The lights in this old town are terrestrial constellations their own fragmented bodies lit fuses. You can begin to see life passing through your fingers, a firework of new skin. A seduction of storytelling, brute mythology, between your ancestral longings you sat with your amnesia in its prime forgetting the moment of your birth and the rains of your death.

Hiss of Paranoia

"4.6% of U.S adults experienced serious mental illness in 2018 (11.4 million people). This represents 1 in 25 adults."   -*NAMI*

Grey smoke recalling a history of lives. I did not see through the changing days how we had become estranged from our very own past. Orion with his hilt of stars reading late in bed. The wandering of memory like strange angels occupied by our own quiescent lives. I thought how we were two strangers that somehow did not quite understand familiarity. Hands like fallen leaves. The next day I woke up and drove among the things that keep the quiet thoughts from banging against the earth. Days like rivers bending in an arc of time. I have been alone waiting for the new moon to put to bed the silence of ghosts whispering magic-madness. The opaque sky and the hiss of paranoia watching over hybrid children of Zion.

Green Wanderings

"Verde Que Te Quiero Verde"   -Federico Garcia Lorca

He had these obscure *presentimientos* about the stasis of my life. Abruptly seeing me in a green field happier than I have ever been then crying emphatically, almost magically into a sea of his hands. Something about that image left its memory marks on my skin like a napkin abruptly pecked with sepia. These are the poems of future tense writing itself an anthology of jade origami herons perhaps. Strange angels walking amongst the living, moving through rooms curious of the lives we live. Wondering about our nature arriving at dusk in the meeting houses of our estranged lovers. The pearly dew of green grass collects into a cistern. We have blindness and a pinkish timbre resonating into the terrestrial hills. Its umber skin growing into the dirt like veins of an acacia tree whispering its mnemonic language of chemistry. These finite hands sinking further into the patterning of odd love-like dreams from some other places. I could venture to touch the singular idea of erasure. The breath being erased slowly by the act of breathing or exhausting its essence because we are made of an amalgamation of time. *Verde* like the jade pinions of flight. A walk-through emerald-green grass bathed in the rains of ichor. Those tacit gods signaling to you from heaven like crosshatching seen up close until that fond semester when you can look out from afar led hand in hand by that docent of fate.

Arrowhead Thoughts

Oversleeping and rolling over into midday
run off settles into a bay of syrupy gossip
amber face in the dark
supine body pivoting on nerves, fuzzy tension
a cradle of hands drawing water to cracked lips, sugary black night
a new era, capillaries of unrelenting isolation: an oracle of trances!
an ode to the void-message
a wall of silence deciphering catastrophe
a messiah of modernity/ a-postmodern-requiem/
years of a pandemic, history writing itself memos to future self:
this seems like the beginning of the end of something big
after the sutures have dissolved
sunflowers climbing lattice paneling
hours count themselves by thoughts,
they are emptying passenger trains letting in an old ghost or two
after years of inebriated witness
nodes of schizophrenia burning, corrosive indigo arrowhead
thoughts dug up from the backyard of childhood
mountains with tiny teeth glaring like ambulance sirens.

Strange Eternities

A new skin soldiering on in an afterlife of waiting and preening. The habits you keep half-starved nudging food towards some new life. Wading in a pool of tempests for a chance to pass down advice for avoidable pain. Sometimes it is a tiny tick festering in the nape or life not giving us want we want. Stammering for when a joke is funny. *Que haces?* A lifetime of call and response. *Que Ma?* We survive in this life, an elevated freeway built over swampland watching out of the windows falling asleep to the Carpenters. On our way to a new home where change is a planet being supervised by the moon's phases. Language as day/night, a dance as each individual kernel within the maracas is a thought dropping from a gum ball machine. A palpable realization that things are ephemeral: we wake up and people are not there to pick up your calls anymore or sit by the table. You look back at memory or the body from where you came, beyond your hair, skin, nails, thoughts and perceive mom/dad/grandma//grandpa. There is a blindness sometimes of worlds we do not live but what was yesterday if only a memory, an imagined place? A dance, a salsa moving alongside a partner as though they were a part of you. You take them home with invisible strings strange eternities inside your womb. Something starts again like a headlamp through a tenuous fog.

Afterthought

A switch flickers clandestine within a half oval change-purse. We wonder at the precocious nature of night happenings circumnavigating wanderings, its serrated jaws filling splendor with two golden teeth separated by natural order. The conviction of wanting stories in your life to funnel through palms sans a hanging bulge of inflamed regrets. A story goes by in a biblical tone of a regret, we did not live, half aware of our history being retold through the lives of strangers. A furrow of skin, this body but smaller merged with other poems written by hands not our own, imagining years running by pooling into a callous; those cagey worrisome mythologies lived by an audience shadowing motion sickness.

Afterthought Cycle

Eyes darting off, wry and estranged denizens of solitude. The skin being plucked from lids, follicles, tiny hairs pried from a womb of natural order like cicada migration after years of sleep to get up and relieve themselves then die. A death like any other death, a life lived like so many nascent custodians of the underworld that have a determined time left alive, a brutality appearing on their scowling jowls. Tides of nude hips where loneliness is a catch-22, underneath a bridge collecting moths with the lucent lick of your body. Stones perish at your touch like phosphorescent girls running down a pack of wolves: that brevity of inertia and now you are the color of water, sacred, sienna or clove, doing merciless works on the sacrum. Just about when morning comes the tiny lights in the bedroom are extinguished and word is no one sleeps in that house but the plants. Having the half-thought of communing with the mycelium between pages of a book that was the laughter of a tree or an ancient language that (infested) Amazonian jungles. If you read the liner notes you forget they're dead. A hospital that carries ghosts to full term or people. The thought trails off and a whisper like a quasar confides in you secrets of your life and you sign a book in some heavenly realm as though confirming something otherworldly that was somehow unpronounceable.

Acknowledgements

Awake, Brevity, PDA like the Half-life of a Plum, Childlike, O' Progeny, Airport/In Transit were published in **Rigorous**.

Mulatto Colony, Ancestral Dysmorphia, Lifecycle of Stars were published in **Ice Colony: What They Leave Behind Anthology**.

Cinema, Invisible Creatures were published in **Coffin Bell Journal**.

Carro Publico was published in **The Closed Eye Open**.

Hopscotch was published in **Untenured Magazine**.

Oracle-bloodline was published in **Punt Volat**.

Afterthought Cycle was published in **Aurora: The Allegory Ridge Poetry Anthology**.

Saffron-touch was published in **Mignolo Arts: Pinky Thinker Issue 5**.

Rivers of Elysium was published in **Wingless Dreamer**.

Abbreviated Space was published in **Landlocked KU Graduate Creative Writing Program**.

Strange Eternities, New Mythology, Green Wanderings, Hard Candy were published in **In Parentheses**.

Catacombs was published in **Kallisto Gaia Press**.

Code Switch was published in **Mortal Mag**.

About Atmosphere Press

Founded in 2015, Atmosphere Press was built on the principles of Honesty, Transparency, Professionalism, Kindness, and Making Your Book Awesome. As an ethical and author-friendly hybrid press, we stay true to that founding mission today.

If you're a reader, enter our giveaway for a free book here:

SCAN TO ENTER
BOOK GIVEAWAY

If you're a writer, submit your manuscript for consideration here:

SCAN TO SUBMIT
MANUSCRIPT

And always feel free to visit Atmosphere Press and our authors online at atmospherepress.com. See you there soon!

Author's Note

HARRY EDGAR PALACIO is an American celebrity, singer-songwriter, writer and artist. He has performed with Grammy winners and Grammy-nominated artists, including Ari Up, lead singer of the Slits; and the 'Godmothers of Punk,' former members of The Raincoats and La Gran Mawon, world renowned Afro-Taino fusion band, at Lucy's Garage; Paramount Theater, NYC; the Dominican Republic; September Fest; Embark; Hudson Valley; and Peekskill, NY. Harry is 'Oregon Kool-aid,' 'Turnstile Eyes,' and 'Harry Edgar Palacio.' His songwriter/ recording artist/ producer projects are found on all platforms. Harry is a multi-award-winning author, including an anthology featured in *Remezcla*, finalist for *Fjords Review* book competition, semi-finalist for *Quartz Literary* competition, grand prix at *Hudson Valley MOCA's Writing the Walls*, Finishing Line Press book competition, and grand prix at St. George School literary contest. He has two books published by Finishing Line Press and this one from Atmosphere Press.

Harry performed at Electronica 1.0 and Electronica 1.1 and has been accepted to be published in *Absurdo Lírio*, *Punt Volat*, *Tule Review*, *LandLocked Magazine*, *Taint Taint Taint Magazine*, *Untenured*, *Inlandia*, and elsewhere. He is an award-winning fine artist with artwork published in *Bellevue Literary Review*, *International Voices*, and more, and has shown fine art at several gallery exhibits in New York City, Westchester, and Hudson Valley, including School of Visual Arts; Peekskill Open Studios 2016, 2017, and 2021; Robeson Gallery; H♥Art Gallery; Crossover XO; Hermosa; and Mount Kisco Arts Council. He was a music journalist and contributor at *Tom Tom Magazine*, *More Sugar*, and *Popfad* music blog.

Harry is the nephew of former Dominican Republic Consulate

José Saldaña. He has read 4,411 books in his lifetime. Harry was the #26 top reader in the US and #49 globally, as well as a WARY 88.1 college radio DJ and rock music director. Harry is an international yoga teacher—200-hour certified by Universe Yoga Alliance in Nepal/ India—and yoga teacher training instructor. His guru is Sri Dharma Mittra (master of poses), who studied under Sri Yogi Gupta. Harry is of second-generation Osho lineage. He has also meditated 118,000 minutes.

Harry, a US citizen, lives in Westchester, New York. He was born in Philadelphia, Pennsylvania. He has former residence in Dominican Republic and Nepal. He received a master's in education from Manhattanville University. Harry was accepted into Harvard University and is an alumni of The New School, *Rolling Stone Magazine*, Parsons School of Design and *Complex*. He is a former New York Military Academy student (JROTC). He is a BIPOC living with schizophrenia.